P9-CQV-787

RED-LETTER PRESS, INC.
SADDLE RIVER, NEW JERSEY

THE BATHROOM INSPIRATION BOOK

ISBN: 0-940462-008

Printed in The United States of America

# INTRODUCTION

"I have had a good many more uplifting thoughts, creative and expansive visions — while soaking in comfortable baths or drying myself after bracing showers — in well-equipped American bathrooms than I have ever had in any cathedral."

Those are the words of literary loo-minary Edmund Wilson (1895-1972). I can't say I agree with Mr. Wilson's assessment because, as publisher of *The Bathroom Inspiration Book*, I staunchly support separation of church and throne. Nonetheless, the bit about having "uplifting thoughts, creative and expansive visions" in the bathroom does hold water. John F. Kennedy, who polished his inaugural address while bathing, would have attested to that. Ditto for Winston Churchill who used to practice addressing The House of Commons while in the bathroom. And musician Franz Schubert who was tuning in the tub when he composed the "Unfinished Symphony."

It is hoped that you too, enhanced by the thought-provoking quotes and off the wall graffiti in *The Bathroom Inspiration Book*, will be richly inspired during your bathroom visits. If so, there's room in the back of this book for your personal "Thoughts From The Throne." But if nothing else, the gems of wit and wisdom gathered by the lavatorial staff of Red-Letter Press will make for some entertaining - and maybe even educational reading while you're perched on the seat of learning.

*Jack Kreismer*
*Publisher*

The Bathroom Library ™

Having children is like having a bowling alley installed in your brain. *—Martin Mull*

* * * *

A real patriot is the fellow who gets a parking ticket and rejoices that the system works. *—Bill Vaughan*

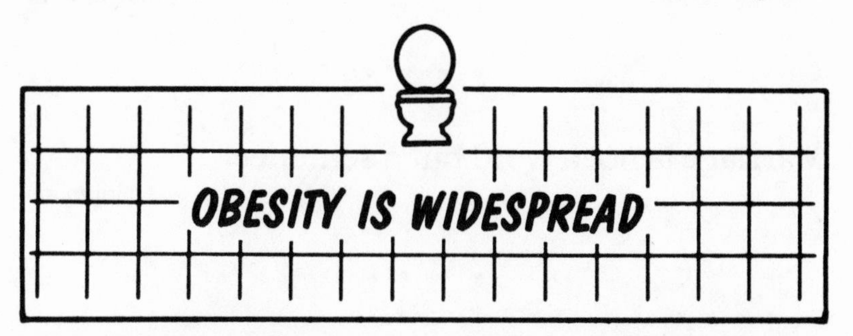


A celebrity is a person who works hard all his life to become known, then wears dark glasses to avoid being recognized. *—Fred Allen*

* * * *

You can observe a lot by watching. *—Yogi Berra*

* * * *

The fence around a cemetery is foolish, for those inside can't come out and those outside don't want to get in. *—Arthur Brisbane*

* * * *

I always wake up at the crack of ice. *—Joe E. Lewis*

Work is a necessity for man. Man invented the alarm clock.
*—Pablo Picasso*

* * * *

There's one way to find out if a man is honest — ask him. If he says "yes" you know he's crooked.
*—Groucho Marx*

* * * *

Marriage is not a word but a sentence.
*—Anonymous*

* * * *

A study of economics usually reveals that the best time to buy anything is last year.
*—Marty Allen*

* * * *

What happens to the hole when the cheese is gone?
*—Bertolt Brecht*

* * * *

Even if you are on the right track, you will get run over if you just sit there.
*—Will Rogers*

* * * *

Wagner's music is better than it sounds.
*—Mark Twain*

If you can't convince them, confuse them.
*—Harry S Truman*

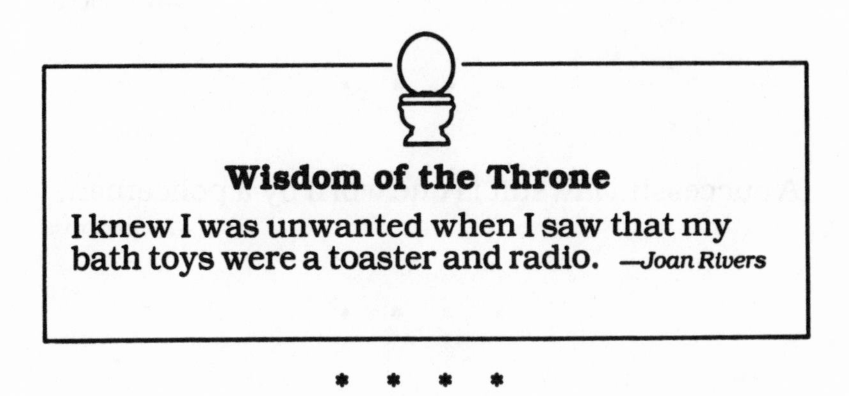

**Wisdom of the Throne**

I knew I was unwanted when I saw that my bath toys were a toaster and radio. *—Joan Rivers*

* * * *

The trouble with burning the candle at both ends is that you always get caught in the middle.
*—Anonymous*

* * * *

I am an idealist. I don't know where I'm going but I'm on my way. *—Carl Sandburg*

* * * *

A straw vote only shows which way the hot air is blowing. *—O. Henry*

* * * *

Whenever I hear people discussing birth control, I always remember that I was the fifth.
*—Clarence Darrow*

If at first you don't succeed, try, try again. Then quit. There's no use being a damn fool about it.

*—W.C. Fields*

* * * *

A successful lawsuit is one worn by a policeman.

*—Robert Frost*

* * * *

The really frightening thing about middle age is the knowledge that you'll outgrow it. *—Doris Day*

* * * *

Never invest your money in anything that eats or needs repainting. *—Billy Rose*

* * * *

Gold is an expensive way of playing marbles.

*—G.K. Chesterton*

* * * *

When Eve saw her reflection in a pool, she sought Adam and accused him of infidelity.

*—Ambrose Bierce*

Do you realize if it weren't for Edison we'd be watching TV by candlelight? —*Al Boliska*

* * * *

People who get down to brass tacks usually rise rapidly. —*Anonymous*

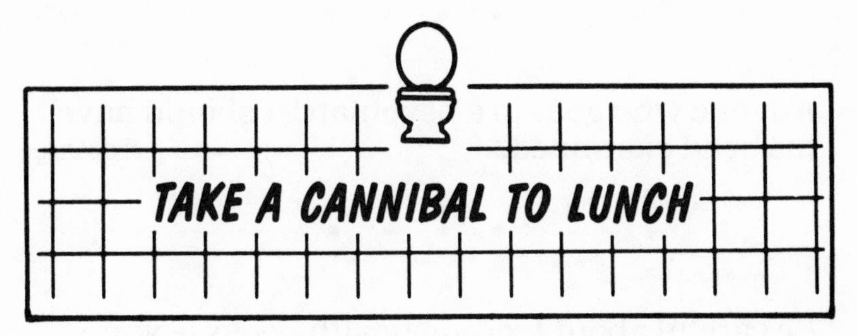


Never go to bed mad. Stay up and fight.
—*Phyllis Diller*

* * * *

The biggest liar in the world is "They Say."
—*Robert Louis Stevenson*

* * * *

Diets are for those who are thick and tired of it.
—*Mary Tyler Moore*

* * * *

Advertising is legalized lying. —*H.G. Wells*

Eighty percent of married men cheat in America. The rest cheat in Europe. *—Jackie Mason*

* * * *

Remember that a kick in the ass is a step forward. *—Anonymous*

* * * *

Anyone who goes to a psychiatrist should have his head examined. *—Samuel Goldwyn*

* * * *

Be careful about reading health books— you might die from a misprint. *—Mark Twain*

* * * *

I can resist everything but temptation. *—Oscar Wilde*

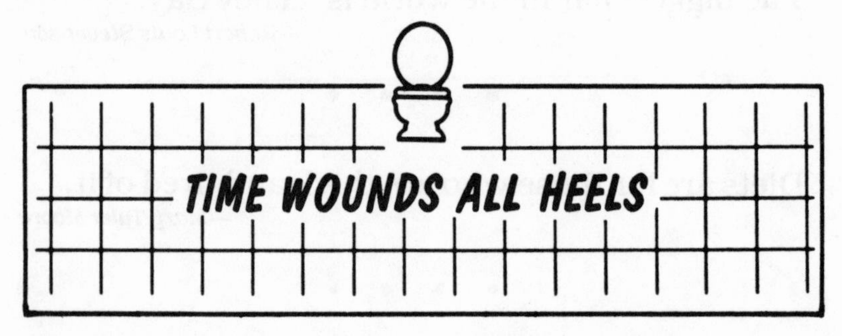


The first requisite for immortality is death. *—Stanislaw Lec*

...kill? He kills for food.
...ently there must be a

*—Woody Allen*

**...n of the Throne**

...untry where the money falls
...ur hands and you can't tear the
...

*—Billy Wilder*

* * * *

A man begins cutting his wisdom teeth the first time he bites off more than he can chew.

*—Herb Caen*

* * * *

When two men in a business always agree, one of them is unnecessary. *—William Wrigley, Jr.*

* * * *

It's hard for me to get used to these changing times. I can remember when the air was clean and sex was dirty. *—George Burns*

* * * *

Ability is the art of getting credit for all the home runs somebody else hits. *—Casey Stengel*

A tourist is a fellow who drives thousands of miles so he can be photographed standing in front of his car.

*—Emile Ganest*

* * * *

All pro athletes are bilingual. They speak English and profanity.

*—Gordie Howe*

* * * *

A conclusion is the place where you get tired of thinking.

*—Martin Fischer*

* * * *

The brain is a wonderful organ; it starts working the moment you get up in the morning and does not stop until you get to the office.

*—Robert Frost*

* * * *

A hair in the head is worth two in the brush.

*—Oliver Herford*

* * * *

Kids are wonderful, but I like mine barbecued.

*—Bob Hope*

I hate a sore winner. —*Oscar Levant*

* * * *

The ballot is stronger than the bullet.
—*Abraham Lincoln*

An archeologist is the best husband a woman can have; the older she gets, the more interested he is in her. —*Agatha Christie*

* * * *

Very few people can afford to be poor.
—*George Bernard Shaw*

* * * *

A man in love is incomplete until he has married. Then he's finished. —*Zsa Zsa Gabor*

* * * *

A fanatic is one who sticks to his guns whether they're loaded or not. —*Franklin P. Jones*

A converted cannibal is one who, on Friday, eats only fishermen.
*—Emily Lotney*

* * * *

Pro football is like nuclear warfare. There are no winners, only survivors.
*—Frank Gifford*

* * * *

The advantage of a classical education is that it enables you to despise the wealth which it prevents you from achieving.
*—Russell Green*

* * * *

In Heaven an angel is nobody in particular.
*—George Bernard Shaw*

* * * *

An arsonist is one with a burning desire.
*—Anonymous*

* * * *

The trouble with the rat race is that even if you win you're still a rat.
*—Lily Tomlin*

A gentleman is someone who is never unintentionally rude. —*Oscar Wilde*

* * * *

When you go into court you are putting your fate into the hands of twelve people who weren't smart enough to get out of jury duty. —*Norm Crosby*

**Wisdom of the Throne**

Fame lost its appeal for me when I went into a public restroom and an autograph seeker handed me a pen and paper under the stall door. —*Marlo Thomas*

* * * *

Genius may have its limitations, but stupidity is not thus handicapped. —*Elbert Hubbard*

* * * *

Statistics are like a bikini. What they reveal is suggestive, but what they conceal is vital. —*Aaron Levenstein*

* * * *

Memory is what makes you wonder what you've forgotten to do. —*Anonymous*

And so we plough along, as the fly said to the ox.
*—Henry Wadsworth Longfellow*

* * * *

Never trust a man with short legs - brains too near their bottoms.
*—Sir Noel Coward*

Have you ever seen a candidate talking to a rich person on television?
*—Art Buchwald*

* * * *

My own business always bores me to death; I prefer other people's.
*—Oscar Wilde*

* * * *

Everything is worth precisely as much as a belch, the difference being that the belch is more satisfying.
*—Ingmar Bergman*

High heels were invented by a woman who had been kissed on the forehead. *—Christopher Morley*

* * * *

Never keep up with the Joneses. Drag them down to your level. *—Quentin Crisp*

* * * *

You can get much farther with a kind word and a gun than you can get with a kind word alone. *—Al Capone*

* * * *

The two most beautiful words in the English language are: "Check enclosed." *—Dorothy Parker*

* * * *

Politics is not a bad profession. If you succeed there are many rewards, if you disgrace yourself you can always write a book. *—Ronald Reagan*

* * * *

A verbal contract isn't worth the paper it's written on. *—Samuel Goldwyn*

* * * *

Usually, the food that you get in art museums is institutional revenge for the art that you get in restaurants. *—Ralph Collier*

After all is said and done, more is said than done.
—*Anonymous*

* * * *

If your doctor warns that you have to watch your drinking, find a bar with a mirror. —*John Mooney*

* * * *

When a man points a finger at someone else, he should remember that four of his fingers are pointing at himself. —*Louis Nizer*

* * * *

Gross ignorance - 144 times worse than ordinary ignorance. —*Bennett Cerf*

* * * *

The thing that impresses me most about America is the way parents obey their children.
—*The Duke of Windsor (Edward VIII of England)*

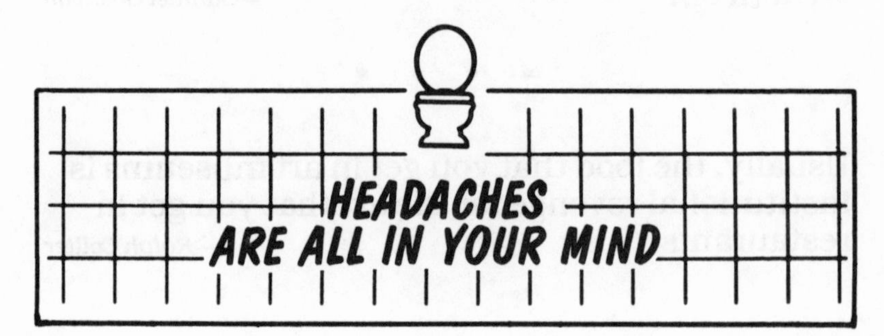

A kleptomaniac is a person who helps himself because he can't help himself. *—Henry Morgan*

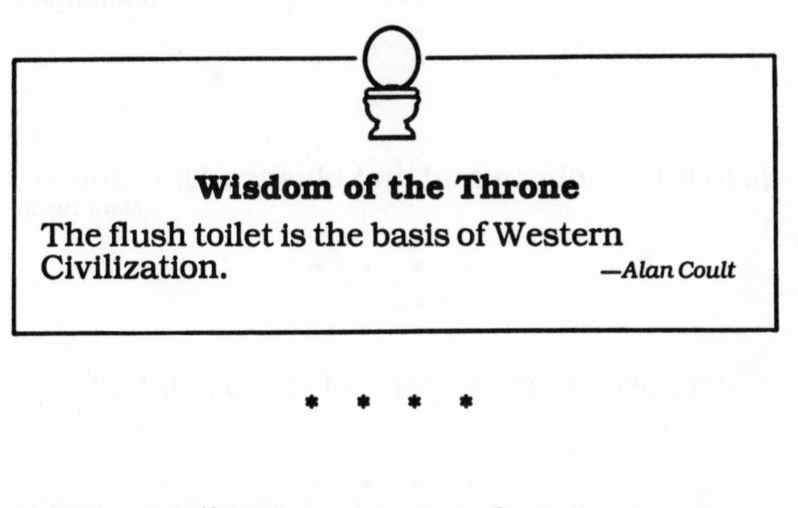

**Wisdom of the Throne**

The flush toilet is the basis of Western Civilization. *—Alan Coult*

* * * *

Military intelligence is a contradiction in terms. *—Groucho Marx*

* * * *

Vote early and vote often. *—Al Capone*

* * * *

Whenever a man's friends begin to compliment him about looking young, he may be sure that they think he is growing old. *—Washington Irving*

* * * *

How holy people look when they are seasick! *—Samuel Butler*

There's no trick to being a humorist when you have the whole government working for you.

*—Will Rogers*

* * * *

Man is the only animal that blushes. Or needs to.

*—Mark Twain*

* * * *

Ninety percent of the game of baseball is half mental.

*—Yogi Berra*

* * * *

Why be disagreeable, when with a little effort you can be impossible?

*—Douglas Woodruff*

* * * *

If there was no faith there would be no living in this world. We couldn't even eat hash with any safety.

*—Josh Billings*

* * * *

The jean. The jean is the destruction. It is the dictator. It is destroying creativity. The jean must be stopped.

*—Pierre Cardin*

As a nation we are dedicated to keeping physically fit - and parking as close to the stadium as possible. —*Bill Vaughan*

* * * *

More than any time in history mankind faces a crossroads. One path leads to despair and utter hopelessness, the other to total extinction. Let us pray that we have the wisdom to choose correctly. —*Woody Allen*

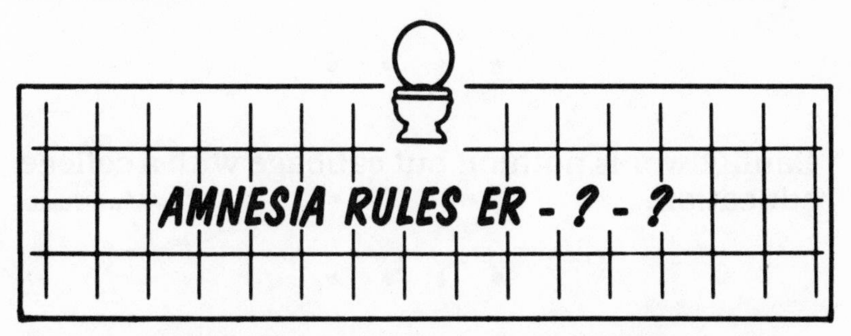


It's a recession when your neighbor loses his job; it's a depression when you lose your own. —*Harry S Truman*

* * * *

No one can feel as helpless as the owner of a sick goldfish. —*Frank McKinney Hubbard*

* * * *

It ain't bragging if you really done it. —*Dizzy Dean*

Punctuality is the thief of time. —*Oscar Wilde*

* * * *

When a man is asked to make a speech, the first thing he has to decide is what to say. —*Gerald Ford*

* * * *

I am free of all prejudices. I hate every one equally. —*W.C. Fields*

* * * *

Cauliflower is nothing but cabbage with a college education. —*Mark Twain*

* * * *

A fanatic is someone who can't change his mind and won't change the subject. —*Winston Churchill*

* * * *

It's hard to be funny when you have to be clean. —*Mae West*

* * * *

If you look like your passport photo, in all probability you need the journey. —*Earl Wilson*

Insomniacs don't sleep because they worry about it, and they worry about it because they don't sleep. *—Franklin Pierce Adams*

* * * *

The meek shall inherit the earth, but not the mineral rights.

*—J. Paul Getty*

* * * *

There are three kinds of lies: lies, damned lies, and statistics.

*—Benjamin Disraeli*

* * * *

I kissed my first woman and smoked my first cigarette on the same day. I have never had time for tobacco since. *—Arturo Toscanini*

* * * *

Some of us are becoming the men we wanted to marry.

*—Gloria Steinem*

I watch a lot of baseball on radio. *—Gerald Ford*

* * * *

Hollywood is a sewer with service from the Ritz Carlton.

*—Wilson Mizner*

* * * *

Money is better than poverty, if only for financial reasons.

*—Woody Allen*

* * * *

If you don't want to work you have to earn enough money so that you won't have to work.

*—Ogden Nash*

* * * *

Ours is a world of nuclear giants and ethical infants.

*—General Omar Bradley*

If I could drop dead right now, I'd be the happiest man alive.

*—Samuel Goldwyn*

* * * *

You can't have everything. Where would you put it?

*—Steven Wright*

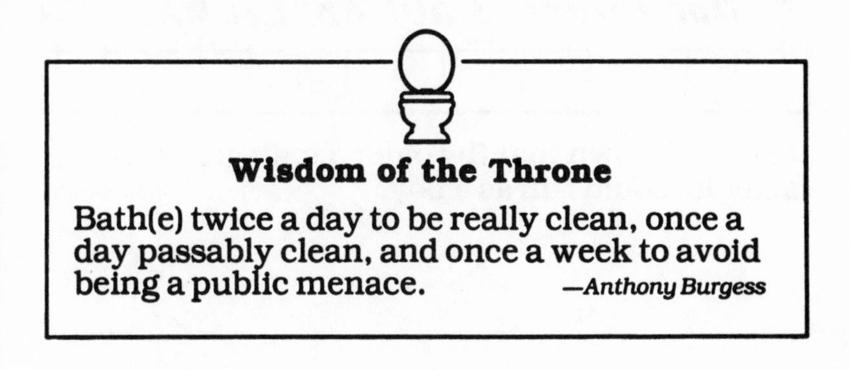

**Wisdom of the Throne**

Bath(e) twice a day to be really clean, once a day passably clean, and once a week to avoid being a public menace.

*—Anthony Burgess*

* * * *

Please accept my resignation. I don't want to belong to any club that will accept me as a member.

*—Groucho Marx*

* * * *

When a man sits with a pretty girl for an hour, it seems like a minute. But let him sit on a hot stove for a minute - and it's longer than any hour. That's relativity.

*—Albert Einstein*

* * * *

A dyspeptic is a man that can eat his cake and have it too.

*—Austin O'Malley*

If the grass is greener in the other fellow's yard - let him worry about cutting it. *—Fred Allen*

It is well known that the older a man grows, the faster he could run as a boy. *—Red Smith*

* * * *

People who think they know everything are very irritating to those of us who do. *—Anonymous*

* * * *

Abstract Art? A product of the untalented, sold by the unprincipled to the utterly bewildered. *—Al Capp*

* * * *

The history of things that didn't happen has never been written. *—Henry Kissinger*

There's no place like home, after the other places close.
*—Anonymous*

* * * *

An atheist is a guy who watches a Notre Dame - S.M.U. football game and doesn't care who wins.
*—Dwight D. Eisenhower*

* * * *

Cannibal - a guy who goes into a restaurant and orders the waiter.
*—Jack Benny*

* * * *

One out of four people in this country is mentally imbalanced. Think of your three closest friends - if they seem okay, then you're the one. *—Ann Landers*

* * * *

Marriage makes an end of many short follies - being one long stupidity.
*—Friedrich Nietzche*

* * * *

That old law about "an eye for an eye" leaves everybody blind.
*—Martin Luther King, Jr.*

People will buy anything that's one to a customer.
—*Sinclair Lewis*

* * * *

I may have my faults, but being wrong ain't one of them.
—*Jimmy Hoffa*

* * * *

Do not do unto others as you would that they should do unto you. Their tastes may not be the same.
—*George Bernard Shaw*

* * * *

I wanted to be the first woman to burn her bra, but it would have taken the fire department four days to put it out.
—*Dolly Parton*

* * * *

Flattery is all right - if you don't inhale.
—*Adlai Stevenson*

* * * *

All animals are equal, but some are more equal than others.
*George Orwell*

One nice thing about egotists - they don't talk about other people. *—Lucille S. Harper*

* * * *

It's hard to keep your shirt on when you're getting something off your chest. *—Nipsey Russell*

**Wisdom of the Throne**

The first thing I do in the morning is brush my teeth and sharpen my tongue. *—Oscar Levant*

* * * *

A neurotic is a man who builds a castle in the air. A psychotic is the man who lives in it. A psychiatrist is the man who collects the rent.
*—Jerome Lawrence*

* * * *

It is better to have loafed and lost than never to have loafed at all. *—James Thurber*

* * * *

Many are called but few get up. *—Oliver Herford*

A perpetual holiday is a good working definition of hell.
*—George Bernard Shaw*

* * * *

Three o'clock is always too late or too early for anything you want to do.
*—Jean-Paul Sartre*

* * * *

A woman is like a teabag. You don't know her strength until she is in hot water.
*—Nancy Reagan*

* * * *

Every family tree has some sap.
*—Anonymous*

* * * *

I think people should go into public office for a term or two, and then get back into their business and live under the laws that they passed.
*—Mike Curb*

* * * *

When you're green, you're growing. When you're ripe, you rot.
*—Ray Kroc*

Although I never played football, I made many contributions. I went to the University of Southern California in the late 1940s and took the English exams for all the Trojan linemen.

*—Art Buchwald*

* * * *

There is a natural hootchy-kootchy to a goldfish.

*—Walt Disney*

'Tis more blessed to give than to receive; for example, wedding presents. *—H.L. Mencken*

* * * *

The illegal we do immediately. The unconstitutional takes a little longer.

*—Henry Kissinger*

* * * *

What a good thing Adam had - when he said a good thing, he knew nobody had said it before.

*—Mark Twain*

A vegetarian is a person who won't eat anything that can have children. —*David Brenner*

* * * *

There is no way to find out why a snorer can't hear himself snore. —*Mark Twain*

**Wisdom of the Throne**

Having two bathrooms ruined the capacity to cooperate. —*Margaret Mead*

* * * *

Too bad that all the people who know how to run the country are busy driving taxicabs and cutting hair. —*George Burns*

* * * *

Drinking makes such fools of people, and people are such fools to begin with, that it's compounding a felony. —*Robert Benchley*

* * * *

A man who is a genius and doesn't know it probably isn't. —*Robert E. Lee*

It is no secret that organized crime in America takes in over forty billion dollars a year. This is quite a profitable sum, especially when one considers that the Mafia spends very little for office supplies. *—Woody Allen*

* * * *

The plural of spouse is spice. *—Christopher Morley*

* * * *

The only difference between a saint and a sinner is that every saint has a past, and every sinner has a future. *—Oscar Wilde*

* * * *

A synonym is a word you use when you can't spell the other one. *—Anonymous*

* * * *

There are two classes of pedestrians in these days of reckless motor traffic: the quick and the dead. *—Lord Dewar*

* * * *

A man will sometimes devote all his life to the development of one part of his body - the wishbone. *—Robert Frost*

Fish and visitors smell in three days.

*—Benjamin Franklin*

* * * *

The best minds are not in the government. If any were, business would hire them away.

*—Ronald Reagan*

* * * *

Wrong telephone numbers are never busy.

*—Anonymous*

* * * *

A man by himself is in bad company. *—Eric Hoffer*

* * * *

Paying alimony is like having the TV set on after you've fallen asleep. *—Henny Youngman*

* * * *

In Czechoslovakia there is no such thing as freedom of the press. In the United States there is no such thing as freedom from the press.

*—Martina Navratilova*

Age is a question of mind over matter. If you don't mind, it doesn't matter. —*Satchel Paige*

* * * *

Give a man a free hand and he'll run it all over you. —*Mae West*

No one has ever had an idea in a dress suit. —*Sir Frederick G. Banting*

* * * *

Men's legs have a terribly lonely life - standing in the dark in your trousers all day. —*Ken Dodd*

* * * *

I'm proud to be paying taxes in the United States. The only thing is - I could be just as proud for half the money. —*Arthur Godfrey*

I'm a Ford, not a Lincoln. *—Gerald R. Ford*

* * * *

Elephants and grandchildren never forget.
*—Andy Rooney*

* * * *

The reason the all-American boy prefers beauty to brains is that the all-American boy can see better than he can think. *—Farrah Fawcett Majors*

* * * *

There's always free cheese in a mousetrap.
*—Anonymous*

* * * *

A lost article invariably shows up after you replace it. *—Calvin Coolidge*

* * * *

Bigamy is having one wife too many. Monogamy is the same. *—Oscar Wilde*

* * * *

To me old age is always fifteen years older than I am. *—Bernard Baruch*

People who like this sort of thing will find this is the sort of thing they like. *—Abraham Lincoln*

* * * *

A fellow who is always declaring he's no fool usually has his suspicions. *—Wilson Mizner*

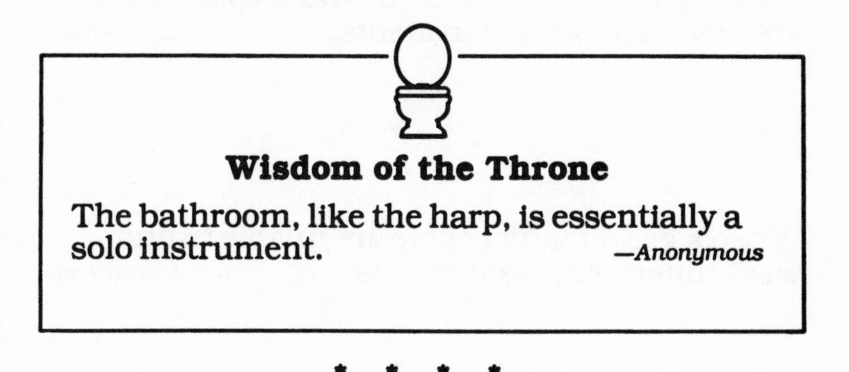

**Wisdom of the Throne**

The bathroom, like the harp, is essentially a solo instrument. *—Anonymous*

* * * *

Women are like elephants to me; I like to look at them, but I wouldn't want to own one. *—W.C. Fields*

* * * *

He who laughs last is usually the last to get the joke. *—Terry Cohen*

* * * *

In God we trust; all others must pay cash.
*—American Saying*

You can never expect anything original from an echo.
*—Anonymous*

* * * *

And, you see, we are living in a world in which all wars are wars of defense. All War Departments are now Defense Departments.
*—George Wald*

* * * *

When a great many people are unable to find work, unemployment results.
*—Calvin Coolidge*

* * * *

Etiquette is getting sleepy in company and not showing it.
*—Hyman Maxwell Berston*

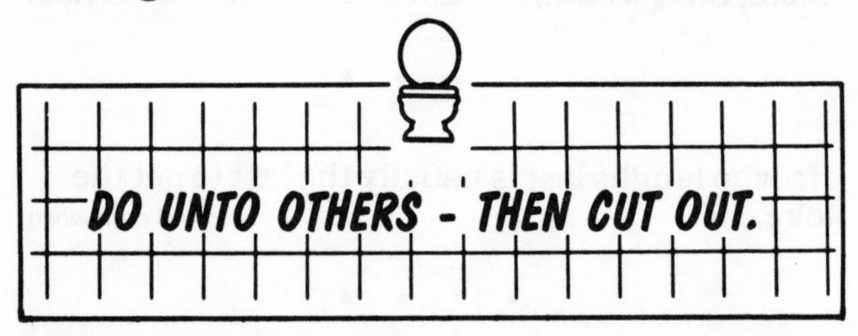


California is a fine place to live in- if you happen to be an orange.
*—Fred Allen*

There is only one consolation in inflation - the money you haven't got isn't worth as much as it used to be.
*—Jack Carter*

* * * *

A self-made man tends to worship his creator.
*—Anonymous*

* * * *

The psychotic says two and two are five and the neurotic knows two and two are four, and hates it.
*—Gordon Gammack*

* * * *

Start every day off with a smile and get it over with.
*—W.C. Fields*

* * * *

I don't believe in an afterlife, although I am bringing a change of underwear.
*—Woody Allen*

* * * *

When I feel like exercising I just lie down until the feeling goes away.
*—Robert M. Hutchins*

The perils of duck hunting are great, especially for the duck. *—Walter Cronkite*

* * * *

Only one man in a thousand is a leader of men - the other 999 follow women. *—Groucho Marx*

* * * *

George Washington never told a lie, but he never had Form 1040 to fill out either. *—Anonymous*

* * * *

Everybody wants to go to heaven, but nobody wants to die. *—Joe Louis*

* * * *

The quickest way of ending a war is to lose it. *—George Orwell*

* * * *

Superstition is foolish, childish, primitive and irrational - but how much does it cost you to knock on wood? *—Judith Viorst*

I'd like to live like a poor man with lots of money.
*—Pablo Picasso*

* * * *

A medium, so called because it is neither rare nor well done. *—Ernie Kovacs*

* * * *

A vacation is what you take when you can no longer take what you've been taking. *—Earl Wilson*

* * * *

Looks are deceiving. A man with a vacant look may have a full house. *—Anonymous*

The only way of catching a train I ever discovered is to miss the train before. *—G.K. Chesterton*

Everything should be made as simple as possible, but not simpler. *—Albert Einstein*

* * * *

Tragedy is if I cut my finger. Comedy is if I walk into an open sewer and die. *—Mel Brooks*

* * * *

A closed mouth gathers no feet. *—American Saying*

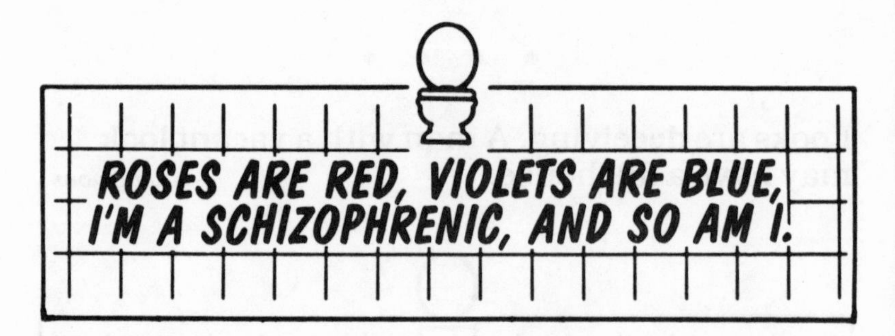


And remember, dearie, never give a sucker an even break. *—W.C. Fields*

* * * *

Have you ever noticed what golf spells backwards? *—Al Boliska*

I have been laid up with intentional flu.

*—Samuel Goldwyn*

* * * *

Middle age is when your old classmates are so grey and wrinkled and bald they don't recognize you. *—Bennett Cerf*

* * * *

Credit buying is much like being drunk. The buzz happens immediately, and it gives you a lift . . . .The hangover comes the day after.

*—Dr. Joyce Brothers*

* * * *

A hole is nothing at all, but you can break your neck in it. *—Austin O'Malley*

* * * *

The trees in Siberia are miles apart - that's why the dogs are so fast. *—Bob Hope*

* * * *

Women prefer men who have something tender about them - especially the legal kind. *—Kay Ingram*

I have noticed that nothing I ever said ever did me any harm. *—Calvin Coolidge*

* * * *

He dreamed he was eating Shredded Wheat and woke up to find the mattress half gone. *—Fred Allen*

* * * *

The best way to study human nature is when nobody else is present. *—Tom Masson*

* * * *

Fishing is a delusion entirely surrounded by liars in old clothes. *—Don Marquis*

* * * *

The wonderful world of home appliances now makes it possible to cook indoors with charcoal and outdoors with gas. *—Bill Vaughan*

* * * *

I never hated a man enough to give him diamonds back.

*—Zsa Zsa Gabor*

We live by the Golden Rule. Those who have the gold make the rules. *—Buzzie Bavasi*

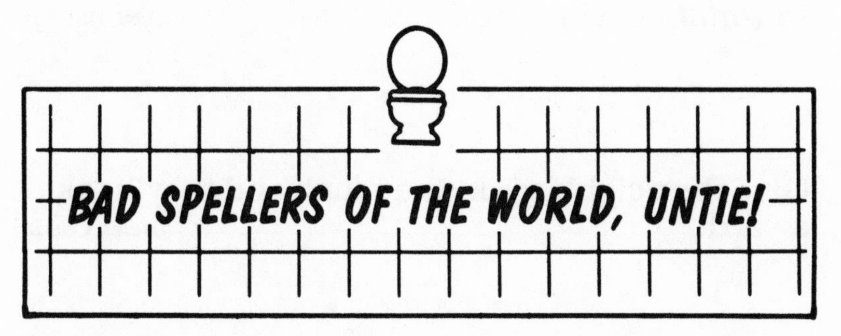


Remember, no one can make you feel inferior without your consent. *—Eleanor Roosevelt*

* * * *

I've been around so long I can remember Doris Day before she was a virgin. *Groucho Marx*

* * * *

To err is human, but when the eraser wears out ahead of the pencil, you're overdoing it. *—J. Jenkins*

* * * *

Even a clock that is not going is right twice a day. *—Polish Proverb*

One of the very best temporary cures for pride and affectation is seasickness. A man who wants to vomit never puts on airs. *—Josh Billings*

* * * *

Give the neighbor's kids an inch and they'll take a yard. *—Helen Castle*

* * * *

To become a professional ice skater you have to practice for hours on end. *—Anonymous*

* * * *

A real executive goes around with a worried look on his assistants. *—Vince Lombardi*

* * * *

It is always the best policy to speak the truth, unless, of course, you are an exceptionally good liar. *—Jerome K. Jerome*

**Wisdom of the Throne**

"When My Love Comes Back from the Ladies' Room Will I Be Too Old to Care?"
*—Lewis Grizzard song title*

There's another advantage of being poor - a doctor will cure you faster. —*Kin Hubbard*

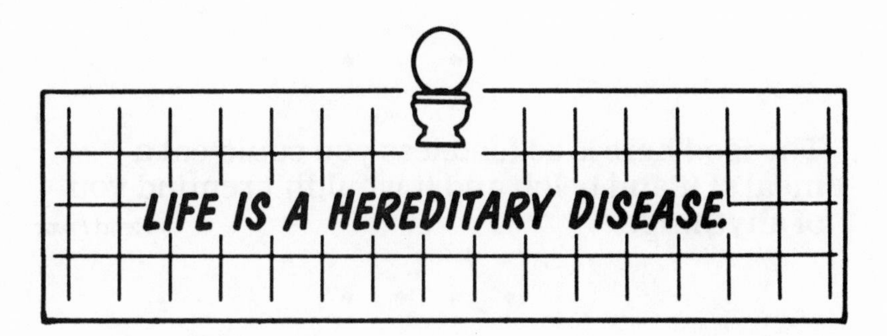


Water taken in moderation cannot hurt anybody.
—*Mark Twain*

* * * *

Never have children, only grandchildren.
—*Gore Vidal*

* * * *

If you can't give me your word of honor, will you give me your promise? —*Samuel Goldwyn*

* * * *

It was one of those parties where you cough twice before you speak, and then decide not to say it after all. —*P.G. Wodehouse*

Middle age is when you've met so many people that every new person you meet reminds you of someone else. *—Ogden Nash*

* * * *

The food here is so tasteless you could eat a meal of it and belch and it wouldn't remind you of anything. *—Redd Foxx*

* * * *

The two biggest sellers in any bookstore are the cookbooks and the diet books. The cookbooks tell you how to prepare the food and the diet books tell you how not to eat any of it. *—Andy Rooney*

* * * *

The nation is prosperous on the whole, but how much prosperity is there in a hole? *—Will Rogers*

* * * *

The early worm get the fishhook. *—Anonymous*

A horse: Dangerous at both ends and uncomfortable in the middle. *—Ian Fleming*

* * * *

Middle age is when you're sitting at home on Saturday night and the telephone rings and you hope it isn't for you. *—Ogden Nash*

I am a believer in punctuality though it makes me very lonely. *—Edward Verral Lucas*

* * * *

You're very foolish if you try to beat around the bush - you just meet yourself coming around the bush the other way. *—Betty Ford*

* * * *

There are no atheists in foxholes.
*—Father William T. Cummings*

It's not really me that's late; it's the others who are always in a hurry. *—Marilyn Monroe*

* * * *

What is my loftiest ambition? I've always wanted to throw an egg into an electric fan. *—Oliver Herford*

* * * *

Our courts' dockets are so crowded today it would be better to refer to it as the overdue process of law. *—Bill Vaughan*

* * * *

Young normal tigers do not eat people. If eaten by a tiger, you may rest assured that he was abnormal. *—Will Cuppy*

* * * *

A critic is a man who knows the way but can't drive the car. *—Kenneth Tynan*

The time to relax is when you don't have time for it.
*—Sydney J. Harris*

* * * *

It was a lucky thing for all of us when Alexander Graham Bell made his first telephone call, the line was not busy.
*—Anonymous*

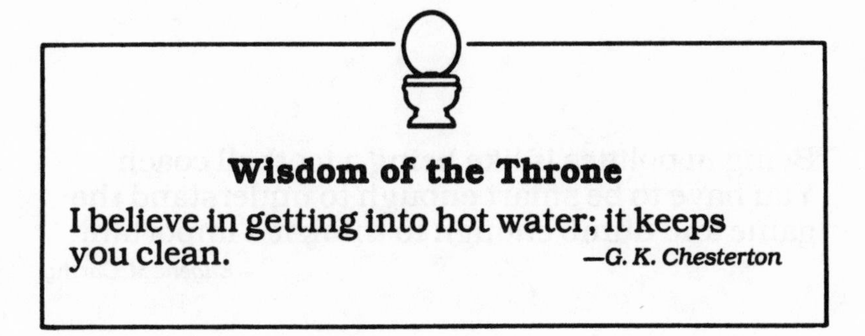

**Wisdom of the Throne**

I believe in getting into hot water; it keeps you clean.
*—G. K. Chesterton*

* * * *

When in doubt, sing loud.
*—Oliver Herford*

* * * *

There is only one cure for grey hair. It was invented by a Frenchman. It is called the guillotine.
*—P. G. Wodehouse*

* * * *

The chicken probably came before the egg because it is hard to imagine God wanting to sit on an egg.
*—Anonymous*

Last night I dreamt I ate a ten-pound marshmallow. When I woke up the pillow was gone.

—*Tommy Cooper*

* * * *

All the Internal Revenue Service wants is what you have left.

—*Anonymous*

* * * *

Being in politics is like being a football coach. You have to be smart enough to understand the game and dumb enough to think it's important.

—*Eugene McCarthy*

Too much of a good thing can be wonderful.

—*Mae West*

* * * *

Courage is walking naked through a cannibal village.

—*Leonard Louis Levenson*

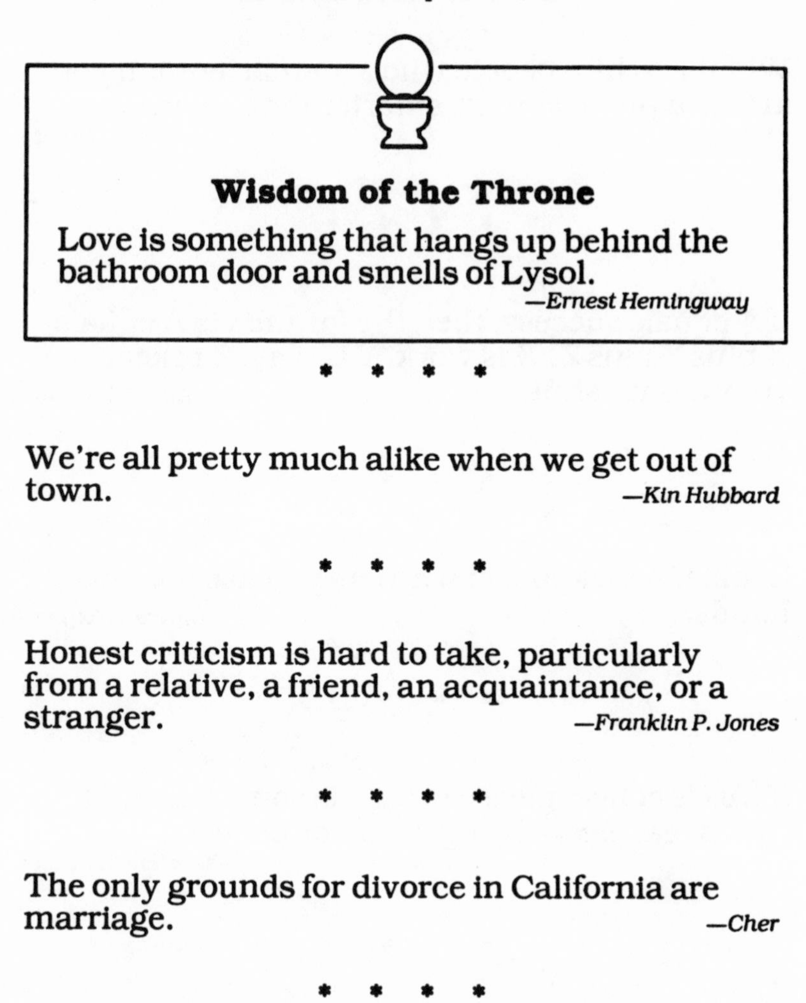

**Wisdom of the Throne**

Love is something that hangs up behind the bathroom door and smells of Lysol.

*—Ernest Hemingway*

* * * *

We're all pretty much alike when we get out of town.

*—Kin Hubbard*

* * * *

Honest criticism is hard to take, particularly from a relative, a friend, an acquaintance, or a stranger.

*—Franklin P. Jones*

* * * *

The only grounds for divorce in California are marriage.

*—Cher*

* * * *

Archie doesn't know how to worry without getting upset.

*—Edith Bunker*

* * * *

As a child, my family's menu consisted of two choices: take it, or leave it.

*—Buddy Hackett*

When you hire people who are smarter than you are, you prove you are smarter than they are.

*—R. H. Grant*

* * * *

If A equals success, then the formula is A equals X plus Y plus Z. X is work. Y is play. Z is keep your mouth shut.

*—Albert Einstein*

* * * *

Bookie: A pickpocket who lets you use your own hands.

*—Henry Morgan*

* * * *

If this is coffee, please bring me some tea: but if this is tea, please bring me some coffee.

*—Abraham Lincoln*

* * * *

I don't like to watch golf on television. I can't stand whispering.

*—David Brenner*

* * * *

There is a great woman behind every idiot.

—John Lennon

If you watch a game, it's fun. If you play it, it's recreation. If you work at it, it's golf. *—Bob Hope*

* * * *

There are two times in a man's life when he should not speculate: when he can't afford it, and when he can. *—Mark Twain*

* * * *

There are moments when everything goes well; don't be frightened, it won't last. *—Jules Renard*

* * * *

Of all the wonders of nature, a tree in summer is perhaps the most remarkable; with the possible exception of a moose singing "Embraceable You" in spats. *—Woody Allen*

Never let a fool kiss you or a kiss fool you. *—Joey Adams*

Always borrow from a pessimist - he never expects to get it back. *—Anonymous*

* * * *

Airline travel is hours of boredom interrupted by moments of stark terror. *—Al Boliska*

* * * *

Retirement takes all the fun out of Saturdays. *—Duke Gmahle*

* * * *

It's the good girls who keep the diaries; the bad girls never have the time. *—Tallulah Bankhead*

* * * *

One of the advantages of bowling over golf is that you very seldom lose a bowling ball. *—Don Carter*

* * * *

You see an awful lot of smart guys with dumb women, but you hardly ever see a smart woman with a dumb guy. *—Erica Jong*

I had a monumental idea this morning, but I didn't like it. —*Samuel Goldwyn*

Trust everybody, but cut the cards.
—*Finley Peter Dunne*

* * * *

More and more these days I find myself pondering on how to reconcile my net income with my gross habits. —*John Kirk Nelson*

* * * *

Russia has abolished God but so far God has been more tolerant. —*John Cameron Swayze*

* * * *

Why do fat chance and slim chance mean the same thing? —*Anonymous*

Beverly Hills is very exclusive. For instance, their fire department won't make house calls.
—*Mort Sahl*

* * * *

Fishing is generally best before you get there or after you leave. —*Anonymous*

* * * *

In suggesting gifts - money is appropriate and one size fits all. —*William Randolph Hearst*

* * * *

Gossip is the art of saying nothing in a way that leaves practically nothing unsaid. —*Walter Winchell*

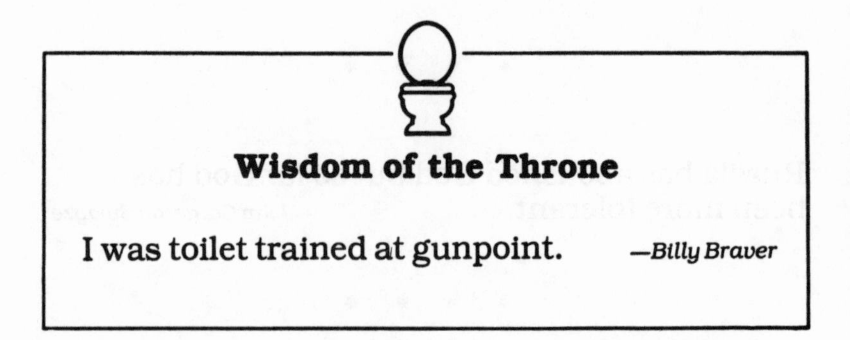


An atheist is a man who has no invisible means of support.
—*Anonymous*

Insanity is hereditary; you can get it from your children.
—*Sam Levenson*

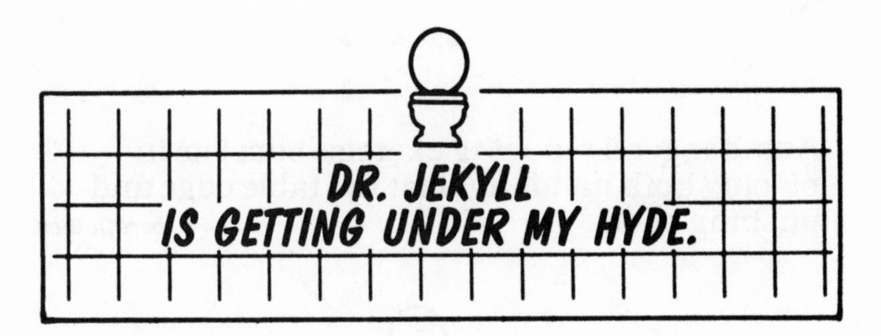


There are plenty of good five-cent cigars in the country. The trouble is they cost a quarter. What this country really needs is a good five-cent nickel.
—*Franklin P. Adams*

* * * *

I shall make electricity so cheap that only the rich can afford to burn candles.
—*Thomas Edison*

* * * *

How can I die? I'm booked.
—*George Burns*

* * * *

If a circus is half as good as it smells, it's a great show.
—*Fred Allen*

Love your neighbor as yourself; but don't take down the fence. —*Carl Sandburg*

* * * *

Another good reducing exercise consists in placing both hands against the table edge and pushing back. —*Robert Quillen*

You can as easily open an oyster without a knife as a lawyer's mouth without a fee. —*American Saying*

* * * *

April 1. This is the day upon which we are reminded of what we are on the other three hundred sixty-four. —*Mark Twain*

* * * *

I just noticed something unusual about my walking: I usually walk in single file. —*Victor Borge*

Macho does not prove mucho. —*Zsa Zsa Gabor*

* * * *

There's no more crime in New York - there's nothing left to steal. —*Henny Youngman*

* * * *

Pickpocket's creed: every crowd has a silver lining. —*Anonymous*

* * * *

Thanks to the Interstate Highway System, it is now possible to travel across the country from coast to coast without seeing anything. —*Charles Kuralt*

* * * *

If you get up early, work late, and pay your taxes, you will get ahead - it you strike oil. —*J. Paul Getty*

* * * *

It's all right letting yourself go, as long as you can let yourself back. —*Mick Jagger*

We prefer the old-fashioned alarm clock to the kind that awakens you with soft music or a gentle whisper. If there's one thing we can't stand early in the morning, it's hypocrisy.

—*Bill Vaughan*

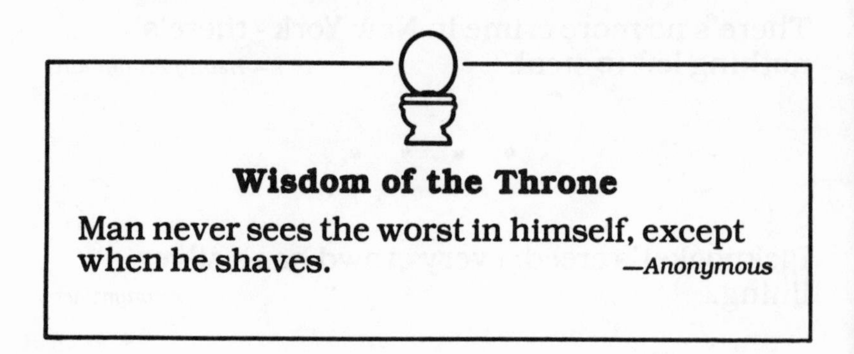

**Wisdom of the Throne**

Man never sees the worst in himself, except when he shaves. —*Anonymous*

* * * *

People need good lies. There are too many bad ones. —*Kurt Vonnegut, Jr.*

* * * *

Include me out. —*Samuel Goldwyn*

* * * *

A fool and his money are soon parted. What I want to know is how they got together in the first place. —*Cyril Fletcher*

* * * *

Never go to a doctor whose office plants have died. —*Erma Bombeck*

There are seventy million books in American libraries, but the one you want to read is always out.
*—Tom Masson*

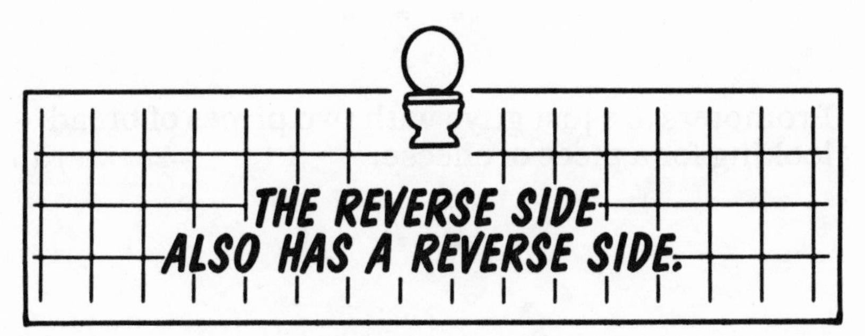


There is one thing about being President - nobody can tell you when to sit down.
*—Dwight D. Eisenhower*

* * * *

If no one dropped out of school, who would hire the college graduates?
*—Anonymous*

* * * *

A liberal is a man too broadminded to take his own side in a quarrel.
*—Robert Frost*

* * * *

If you don't go to other men's funerals they won't go to yours.
*—Clarence Day*

Most of the time I don't have much fun. The rest of the time I don't have any fun at all. —*Woody Allen*

* * * *

Promoters are just guys with two pieces of bread looking for a piece of cheese. —*Evel Knievel*

* * * *

Lack of money is the root of all evil.
—*George Bernard Shaw*

* * * *

Brevity is the soul of lingerie. —*Dorothy Parker*

* * * *

A road map is something that tells you everything you need to know except how to fold it up again.
—*Anonymous*

Exercise is bunk. If you are healthy, you don't need it: if you are sick, you shouldn't take it.

*—Henry Ford*

**Wisdom of the Throne**

I find I always have to write SOMETHING on a steamed mirror.

*—Elaine Dundy*

Some who are not paid what they are worth ought to be glad.

*—Anonymous*

* * * *

Statistics indicate that, as a result of overwork, modern executives are dropping like flies on the nation's golf courses.

*—Ira Wallach*

* * * *

I get no respect. The way my luck is running, if I was a politician I'd be honest.

*—Rodney Dangerfield*

* * * *

Why does a woman work ten years to change a man's habits and then complain that he's not the man she married?

*—Barbara Streisand*

The trouble with life in the fast lane is that you get to the other end in an awful hurry. *—John Jensen*

* * * *

The best part of the fiction in many novels is the notice that the characters are purely imaginary. *—Franklin P. Adams*

* * * *

Venice would be a fine city if it were only drained. *—Ulysses S. Grant*

* * * *

There are a terrible lot of lies going about the world, and the worst of it is that half of them are true. *—Winston Churchill*

* * * *

I have always thought of a dog lover as a dog that was in love with another dog. *—James Thurber*

* * * *

I like a woman with a head on her shoulders. I hate necks. *—Steve Martin*

I don't want any yes-men around me. I want everybody to tell me the truth even if it costs them their jobs.
*—Samuel Goldwyn*

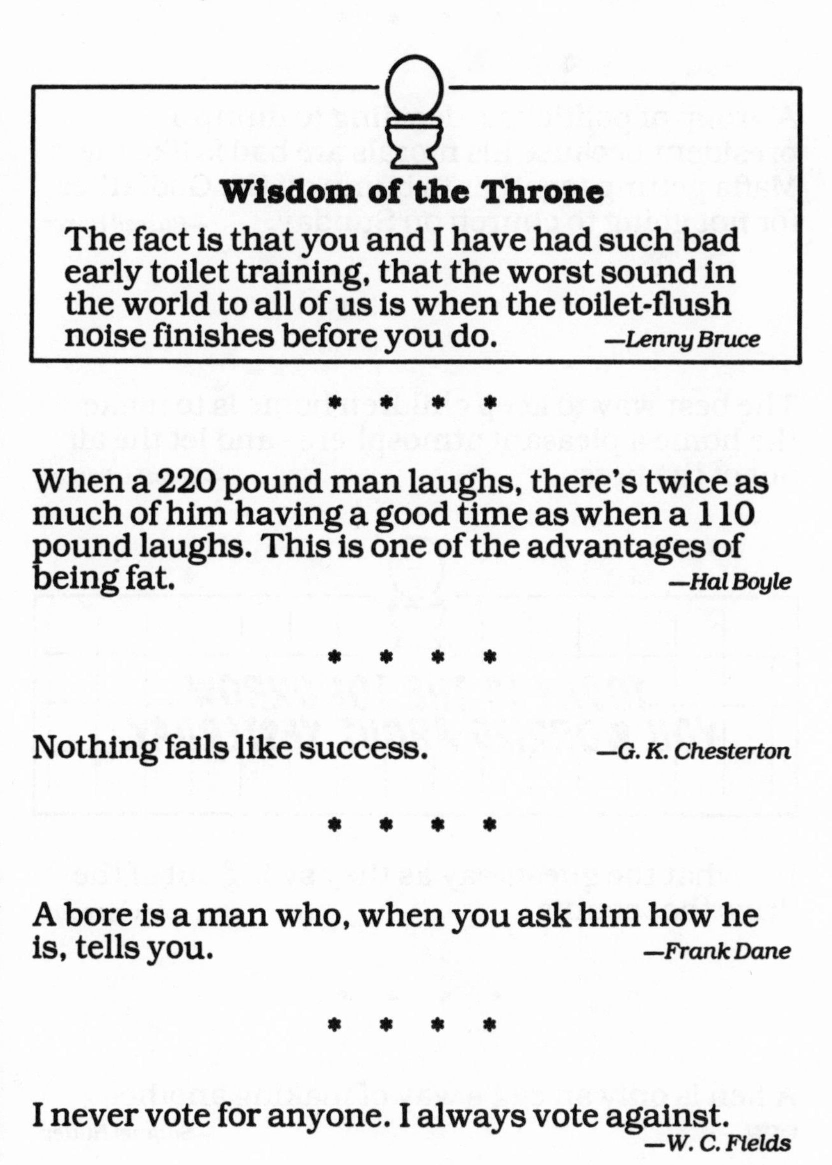

**Wisdom of the Throne**

The fact is that you and I have had such bad early toilet training, that the worst sound in the world to all of us is when the toilet-flush noise finishes before you do.
*—Lenny Bruce*

* * * *

When a 220 pound man laughs, there's twice as much of him having a good time as when a 110 pound laughs. This is one of the advantages of being fat.
*—Hal Boyle*

* * * *

Nothing fails like success.
*—G. K. Chesterton*

* * * *

A bore is a man who, when you ask him how he is, tells you.
*—Frank Dane*

* * * *

I never vote for anyone. I always vote against.
*—W. C. Fields*

The first hundred years are the hardest.

*—Wilson Mizner*

* * * *

A group of politicians deciding to dump a president because his morals are bad is like the Mafia getting together to bump off the Godfather for not going to church on Sunday. *—Russell Baker*

* * * *

The best way to keep children home is to make the home a pleasant atmosphere - and let the air out of the tires. *—Dorothy Parker*

It's what the guests say as they swing out of the drive that counts. *—Anonymous*

* * * *

A hen is only an egg's way of making another egg. *—Samuel Butler*

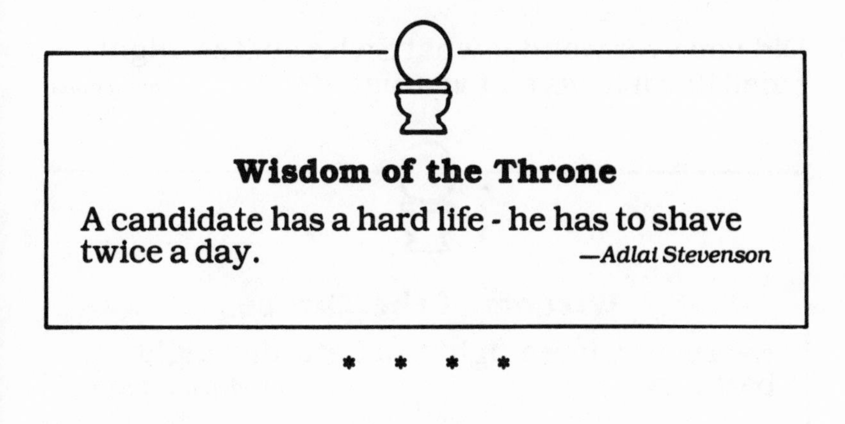

**Wisdom of the Throne**

A candidate has a hard life - he has to shave twice a day. —*Adlai Stevenson*

* * * *

In the old days U.S. Grant meant a famous soldier and not foreign aid. —*Anonymous*

* * * *

If you don't say anything, you won't be called on to repeat it. —*Calvin Coolidge*

* * * *

They are doing things on the screen these days that the French don't even put on postcards. —*Bob Hope*

* * * *

Everybody is ignorant, only on different subjects. —*Will Rogers*

Did you ever wonder what Swiss cheese might smell like if it weren't ventilated? *—Anonymous*

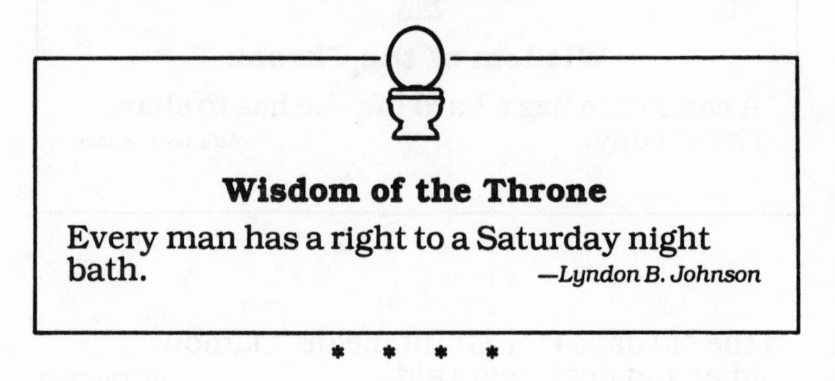

**Wisdom of the Throne**

Every man has a right to a Saturday night bath. *—Lyndon B. Johnson*

* * * *

The handwriting on the wall may be a forgery. *—Ralph Hodgsen*

* * * *

My idea of courage is the guy who has $500,000 tied up in the stock market and turns to the box scores first. *—Earl Wilson*

* * * *

Everyone should keep someone else's diary. *—Oscar Wilde*

* * * *

Early to rise and to bed makes a male healthy and wealthy and dead. *—James Thurber*

There are four things that are overrated in this country: hot chicken soup, sex, the FBI, and parking your car in your garage. *—Erma Bombeck*

* * * *

Being with a woman all night never hurt no professional baseball player. It's staying up all night looking for a woman that does him in.
*—Casey Stengel*

* * * *

It is only possible to live happily ever after on a day to day basis. *—Margaret Bonnano*

* * * *

I've written some poetry I don't understand myself. *—Carl Sandburg*

* * * *

You never realize how short a month is until you pay alimony. *—John Barrymore*

* * * *

A boy can learn a lot from a dog: obedience, loyalty, and the importance of turning around three times before lying down. *—Robert Benchley*

I would have made a good pope. —*Richard Nixon*

* * * *

Live together like brothers and do business like strangers. —*Arab Proverb*

* * * *

I never read a book before reviewing it; it prejudices one so. —*Sydney Smith*

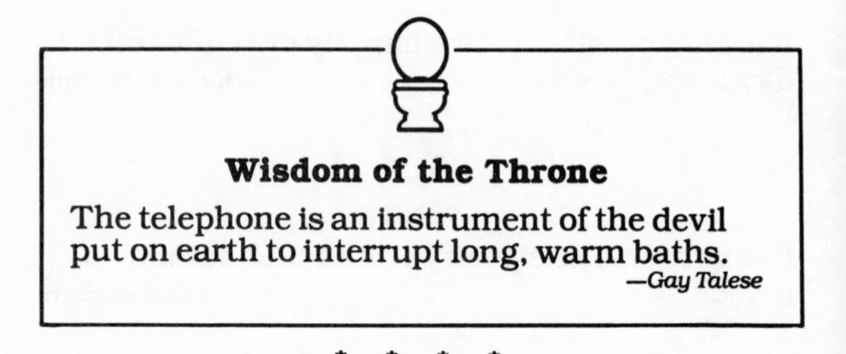

**Wisdom of the Throne**

The telephone is an instrument of the devil put on earth to interrupt long, warm baths. —*Gay Talese*

* * * *

He who hesitates misses the green light, gets bumped in the rear, and loses his parking place. —*Anonymous*

* * * *

It's so beautifully arranged on the plate - you know someone's fingers have been all over it. —*Julia Child*

It is a good thing that life is not as serious as it seems to a waiter. *—Don Herold*

If you're going to do something tonight that you'll be sorry for tomorrow morning, sleep late.
*—Henny Youngman*

* * * *

Why is it that the first gray hairs stick straight out? *—Kin Hubbard*

* * * *

Those who can, do; those who can't teach.
*—George Bernard Shaw*

* * * *

We're all in this alone. *—Lily Tomlin*

I am a deeply superficial person. *—Andy Warhol*

* * * *

There's somebody at every dinner party who eats all the celery. *—Kin Hubbard*

**Wisdom of the Throne**

We've got a problem. Luis Tiant wants to use the bathroom and it says no foreign objects in the toilet. *—Baseball's Graig Nettles, during a New York Yankees' airplane trip*

* * * *

Give a landlord an inch and he'll build an apartment house. *—American Saying*

* * * *

I always say beauty is only sin deep. *—Saki (H. H. Munro)*

A curved line is the loveliest distance between two points.
—*Mae West*

A "woman driver" is one who drives like a man and gets blamed for it.
—*Patricia Ledger*

* * * *

Confucius say: Success give man big head, also big belly.
—*Anonymous*

* * * *

Let us all be happy and live within our means, even if we have to borrow the money to do it with.
—*Artemus Ward*

* * * *

If you drink like a fish, don't drive. Swim.
—*Joe E. Lewis*

Coward: One who in a perilous emergency thinks with his legs.
*—Ambrose Bierce*

* * * *

Man is the animal that intends to shoot himself out into interplanetary space, after having given up on the problem of an efficient way to get himself five miles to work and back each day.
*—Bill Vaughan*

* * * *

Humor is falling downstairs if you do it while in the act of warning your wife not to.
*—Kenneth Bird*

* * * *

A mine is a hole in the ground owned by a liar.
*—Mark Twain*

* * * *

In baiting a mousetrap with cheese, always leave room for the mouse.
*—Saki (H. H. Munro)*

* * * *

Doctors are just the same as lawyers; the only difference is that lawyers merely rob you, whereas doctors rob you and kill you, too.
*—Anton Chekhov*

A lie is an abomination unto the Lord and a very present help in time of trouble. —*Adlai Stevenson*

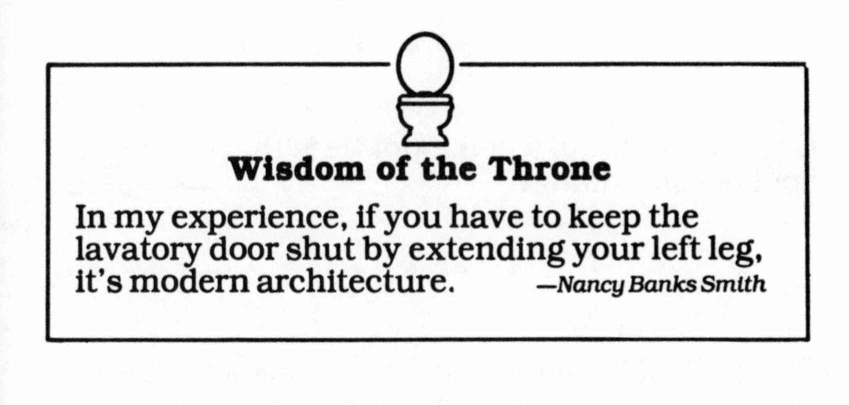

**Wisdom of the Throne**

In my experience, if you have to keep the lavatory door shut by extending your left leg, it's modern architecture. —*Nancy Banks Smith*

* * * *

There cannot be a crisis next week. My schedule is already full. —*Henry Kissinger*

* * * *

An elephant never forgets - but then what has he got to remember? —*Anonymous*

* * * *

I've learned that any kid will run any errand for you, if you ask at bedtime. —*Red Skelton*

What the world needs is more geniuses with humility, there are so few of us left. *—Oscar Levant*

* * * *

One advantage of a polka-dot tie is that one more spot doesn't matter. *—Anonymous*

* * * *

We can't all be heroes, because somebody has to sit on the curb and clap as they go by. *—Will Rogers*

* * * *

A cynic is a man who, when he smells flowers, looks around for a coffin. *—H. L. Mencken*

* * * *

A narcissist is someone better looking than you are. *—Gore Vidal*

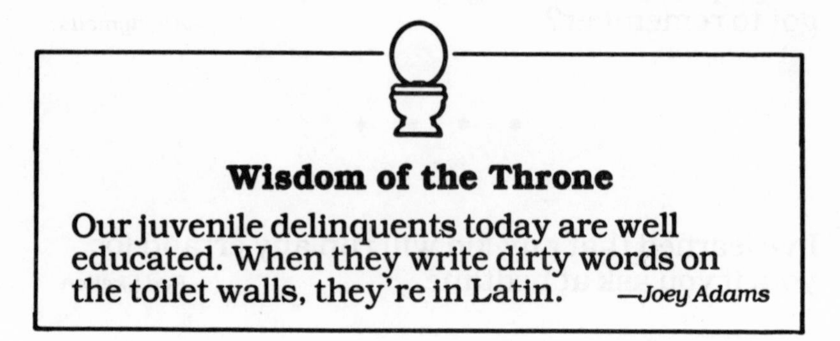

**Wisdom of the Throne**

Our juvenile delinquents today are well educated. When they write dirty words on the toilet walls, they're in Latin. *—Joey Adams*

Seeing is deceiving. It's eating that's believing.
*—James Thurber*

* * * *

A committee is a group that keeps minutes and loses hours.
*—Milton Berle*

All generalizations are false, including this one.
*—Anonymous*

* * * *

A billion dollars is not what it used to be.
*—Bunker Hunt*

* * * *

The more you read and observe about this politics thing, you got to admit that each party is worse than the other. The one that's out always looks the best.
*– Will Rogers*

We all get the same amount of ice. The rich get it in summertime and the poor get it in winter.

—*Anonymous*

* * * *

Art consists in drawing the line somewhere.

—*G. K. Chesterton*

* * * *

You've heard of the three ages of man: youth, middle age, and "you're looking wonderful!"

—*Cardinal Spellman*

* * * *

No matter how bad things get you got to go on living, even if it kills you.

—*Sholom Aleichem*

* * * *

One should always play fairly when one has the winning cards.

—*Oscar Wilde*

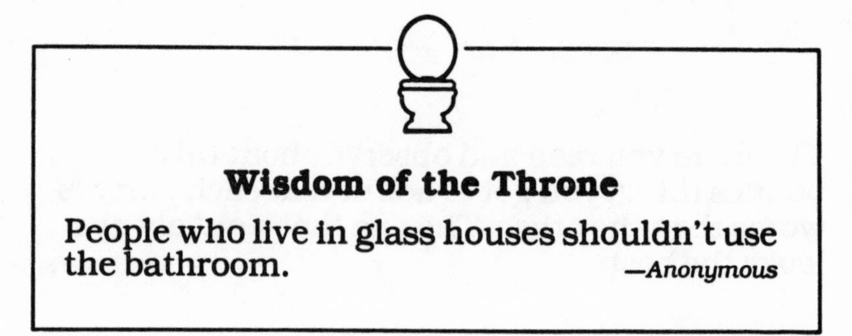

**Wisdom of the Throne**

People who live in glass houses shouldn't use the bathroom.

—*Anonymous*

If you read a lot of books, you're considered well-read. But if you watch a lot of TV, you're not considered well-viewed. *—Lily Tomlin*

* * * *

Business will be better or worse. *—Calvin Coolidge*

Parents were invented to make children happy by giving them something to ignore. *—Ogden Nash*

* * * *

Confidence is simply that quiet, assured feeling you have before you fall flat on your face.
*—Dr. L. Binder*

* * * *

It is bad luck to fall out of a thirteenth-floor window on Friday. *—Anonymous*

A tie (game) is like kissing your sister. *—Bear Bryant*

* * * *

An optimist is a fellow who believes a housefly is looking for a way to get out. *—George Jean Nathan*

* * * *

Television is an invention that permits you to be entertained in your living room by people you wouldn't have in your home. *—David Frost*

* * * *

Don't jump on a man unless he's down.
*—Finley Peter Dunne*

I like work; it fascinates me. I can sit and look at it for hours. *—Jerome K. Jerome*

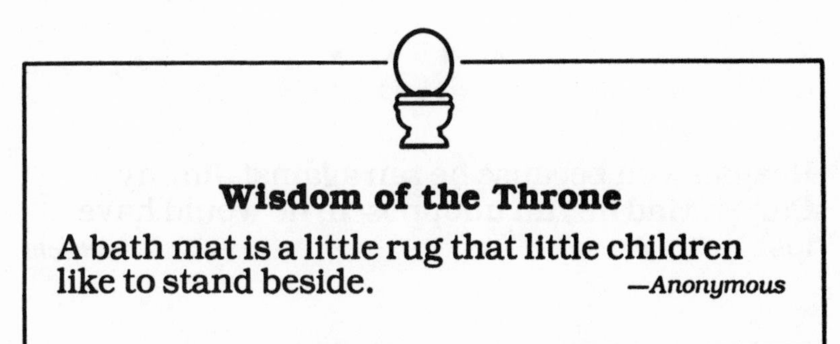

**Wisdom of the Throne**

A bath mat is a little rug that little children like to stand beside. *—Anonymous*

This make me so sore it gets my dandruff up. *—Samuel Goldwyn*

* * * *

Either this man is dead or my watch has stopped. *—Groucho Marx*

* * * *

Horatio Alger started by shining shoes and within one year made a million dollars. He must have used very little polish. *—Sam Levenson*

* * * *

Youth is such a wonderful thing. What a crime to waste it on children. *—George Bernard Shaw*

Where there's a will, there's a lawsuit.

*—Addison Mizner*

* * * *

Reagan won because he ran against Jimmy Carter. Had he run unopposed, he would have lost.

*—Mort Sahl*

* * * *

Interest your kids in bowling. Get them off the streets and into the alleys.

*—Don Rickles*

* * * *

When people are free to do as they please, they usually imitate each other.

*—Eric Hoffer*

One loss is good for the soul. Too many losses is not good for the coach.

*—Knute Rockne*

I find television very educating. Every time somebody turns on the set I go into the other room and read a book. —*Groucho Marx*

* * * *

About the time you catch up with the Joneses, they refinance. —*Anonymous*

**Wisdom of the Throne**

We must have respect for both our plumbers and our philosophers or neither our pipes or our theories will hold water. —*John W. Gardner*

* * * *

The soup is never hot enough if the waiter can keep his thumb in it. —*William Collier*

* * * *

The only reason I would take up jogging is so that I could hear heavy breathing again. —*Erma Bombeck*

Sometimes when I look at all my children, I say to myself, "Lillian, you should have stayed a virgin."
*—Lillian Carter*

* * * *

I don't care what is written about me so long as it isn't true.
*—Katharine Hepburn*

* * * *

One of the things you can still get for a nickel is a penny's worth of time on a parking meter.
*—Anonymous*

* * * *

If lawyers are disbarred and clergymen defrocked, doesn't it follow that electricians can be delighted; musicians denoted; cowboys deranged; models deposed; tree surgeons debarked and dry cleaners depressed?
*—Virginia Ostman*

If I were two-faced, would I be wearing this one?
*—Abraham Lincoln*

It often happens that I wake at night and begin to think about a serious problem and decide I must tell the Pope about it. Then I wake up completely and remember that I am the Pope. *—Pope John XXIII*

* * * *

If the people don't want to come out to the park, nobody's going to stop 'em. *—Yogi Berra*

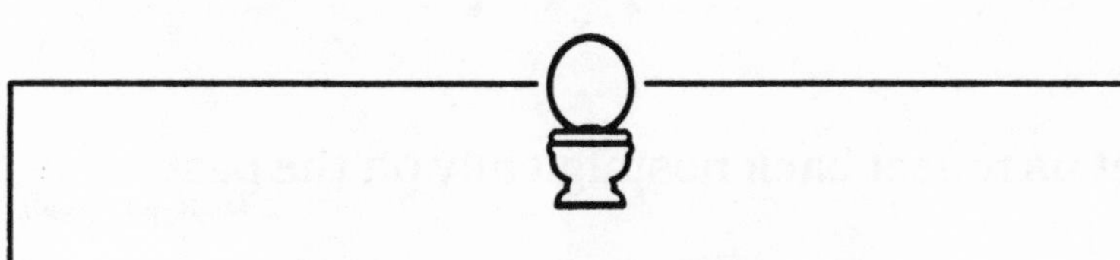

**Wisdom of the Throne**

I stay there for hours. Sometimes I even fill it with water. *—Woody Allen, on relaxing in a tub*

* * * *

When small men begin to cast big shadows, it means that the sun is about to set. *—Lin Yutang*

* * * *

The trouble with being punctual is that nobody's there to appreciate it. *—Franklin P. Jones*

In spite of the cost of living, it's still popular.

—*Kathleen Norris*

* * * *

Let us reflect back nostalgically on the past.

—*Howard Cosell*

* * * *

No matter how thin you slice it, it's still baloney.

—*Rube Goldberg*

* * * *

We lived for days on nothing but food and water.

—*W. C. Fields*

* * * *

Dying is one of the few things that can be done as easily lying down.

—*Woody Allen*

They say you can't do it, but sometimes it doesn't always work.

*—Casey Stengel*

* * * *

Never put off till tomorrow what you can do the day after tomorrow.

*—Mark Twain*

* * * *

I've a grand memory for forgetting.

*—Robert Louis Stevenson*

* * * *

When you're down and out something always turns up - and it is usually the noses of your friends.

*—Orson Welles*

* * * *

It is better to be looked over than overlooked.

*—Mae West*

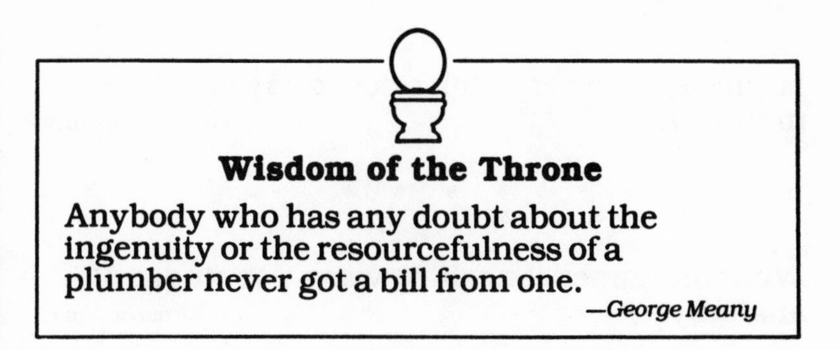

**Wisdom of the Throne**

Anybody who has any doubt about the ingenuity or the resourcefulness of a plumber never got a bill from one.

*—George Meany*

Keep running after a dog and he will never bite you.
—*François Rabelais*

* * * *

Very few people do anything creative after the age of thirty-five. The reason is that very few people do anything creative before the age of thirty-five.
—*Joel Hildebrand*

When a man wants to murder a tiger he calls it sport; when a tiger wants to murder him he calls it ferocity.
—*George Bernard Shaw*

* * * *

I think age is a very high price to pay for maturity.
—*Tom Stoppard*

* * * *

Whoever named it necking was a poor judge of anatomy.
—*Groucho Marx*

The big shots are only the little shots who keep on shooting. —*Christopher Morley*

* * * *

Asthma doesn't seem to bother me any more unless I'm around cigars or dogs. The thing that would bother me most would be a dog smoking a cigar. —*Steve Allen*

* * * *

Progress might have been all right once but it has gone on too long. —*Ogden Nash*

* * * *

A diplomat is one who can tell a man he's open-minded when he means he has a hole in his head. —*Anonymous*

* * * *

Somebody must take a chance. The monkeys who did became men, and the monkeys who didn't are still jumping around in trees making faces at the monkeys who did. —*Lincoln Steffens*

* * * *

God may help those who help themselves, but the courts are rough as hell on shoplifters. —*Leo Rosten*

There are terrible temptations which it requires strength and courage to yield to. —*Oscar Wilde*

Some Americans need hyphens in their name because only part of them has come over.

—*Woodrow Wilson*

* * * *

Did you ever have the measles, and if so, how many? —*Artemus Ward*

* * * *

You know you're getting old when the candles cost more than the cake. —*Bob Hope*

* * * *

Watermelon: a good fruit - you eat, you drink and you wash your face. —*Enrico Caruso*

Most people spend their lives going to bed when they're not sleepy and getting up when they are.

*—Cindy Adams*

* * * *

America is a country where they lock up juries and let the defendants out. *—Anonymous*

* * * *

Nobody has ever bet enough on the winning horse. *—Anonymous*

* * * *

A drama critic is a man who leaves no turn unstoned. *—George Bernard Shaw*

I hate television. I hate it as much as peanuts. But I can't stop eating peanuts. *—Orson Welles*

We're overpaying him, but he's worth it.
*—Samuel Goldwyn*

* * * *

When we got into office, the thing that surprised me most was to find that things were just as bad as we'd been saying they were. *—John F. Kennedy*

* * * *

The closest to perfection a person ever comes is when he or she fills out a job application form.
*—Stanley J. Randall*

Why is not a rat as good as a rabbit? Why should men eat shrimp and neglect cockroaches?
*—Henry Ward Beecher*

* * * *

We don't want inflation and we don't want deflation. What we want is flation. *—Anonymous*

If at first you don't succeed, so much for skydiving.

*—Anonymous*

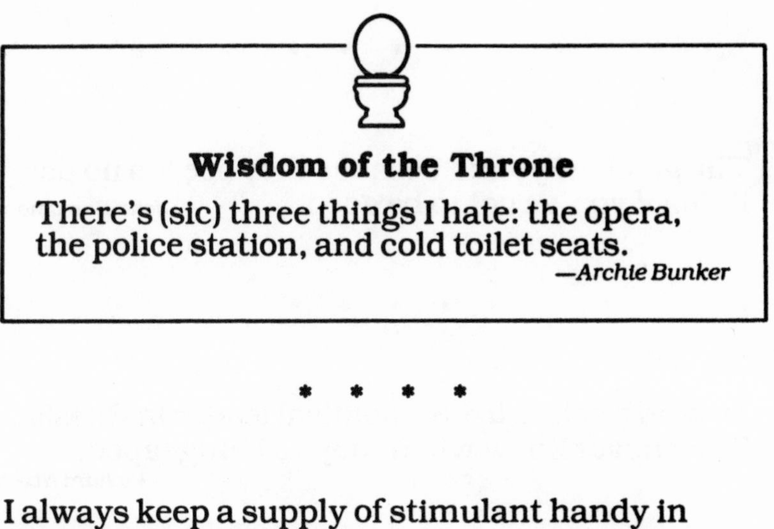

**Wisdom of the Throne**

There's (sic) three things I hate: the opera, the police station, and cold toilet seats.

*—Archie Bunker*

* * * *

I always keep a supply of stimulant handy in case I see a snake - which I also keep handy.

*—W. C. Fields*

* * * *

Fashion is a form of ugliness so intolerable that we have to alter it every six months.

*—Oscar Wilde*

* * * *

The trouble with telling a good story is that it invariably reminds the other fellow of a dull one.

*—Sid Caesar*

* * * *

Nothing is free. Even age. Age is the fee God charges for life.

*—Anonymous*

There is no sweeter sound than the crumbling of one's fellow man. —*Groucho Marx*

* * * *

The good die young because they see it's no use living if you've got to be good. —*John Barrymore*

* * * *

I would not like to be a political leader in Russia. They never know when they're being taped. —*Richard Nixon*

* * * *

The suburbs were discovered quite by accident one day in the early 1940s by a Welcome-Wagon lady who was lost. —*Erma Bombeck*

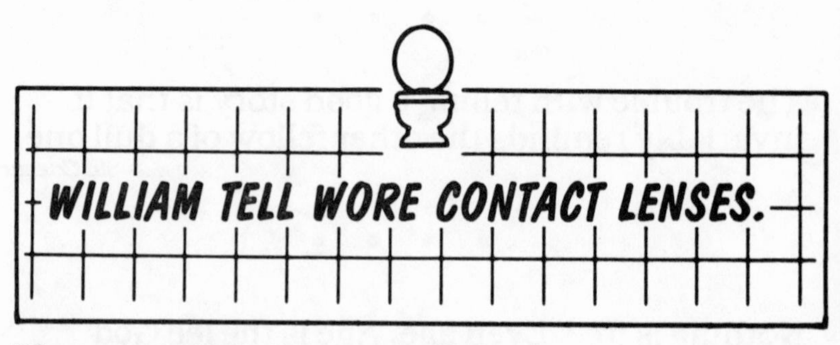


Blooming idiots have no off season. —*Anonymous*

Let's kill all the lawyers. —*William Shakespeare*

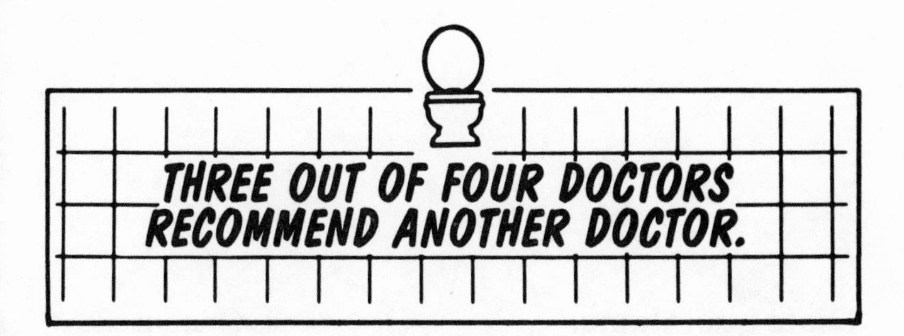


Try the Andy Warhol New York City Diet: when I order in a restaurant, I order everything I don't want, so I have a lot to play around with while everyone else eats. —*Andy Warhol*

* * * *

If you drink, don't drive. Don't even putt.
—*Dean Martin*

* * * *

I go for two kinds of men. The kind with muscles, and the kind without. —*Mae West*

* * * *

You can make a fortune if you know the exact moment when a piece of junk becomes an antique. —*Anonymous*

**I hate quotations.** *—Ralph Waldo Emerson*

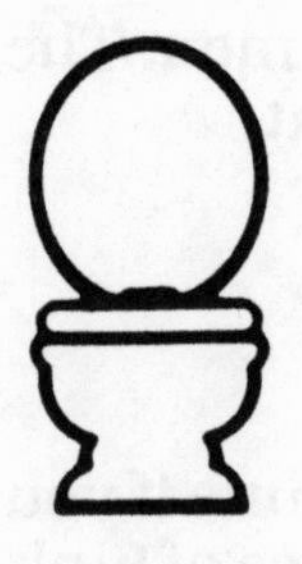

Thoughts From The Throne
Write your own Bathroom Inspired Gems on these pages:

# The Bathroom Library

THE BATHROOM SPORTS QUIZ BOOK
THE BATHROOM ENTERTAINMENT BOOK
THE BATHROOM TRIVIA BOOK
THE BATHROOM DIGEST
THE BATHROOM CROSSWORD PUZZLE BOOK
THE BATHROOM GUEST BOOK
THE BATHROOM GAME BOOK
THE BATHROOM INSPIRATION BOOK



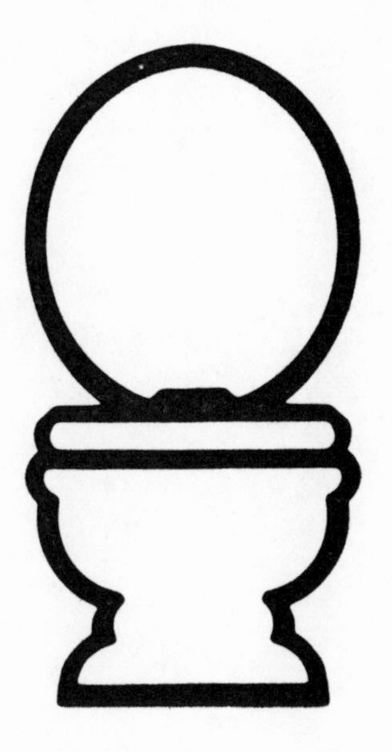